TWELVE DISHES
of Christmas

> A Collection of Holiday Memories and Recipes

Denise Weaver

Copyright © 2023 Denise Weaver
All Rights Reserved

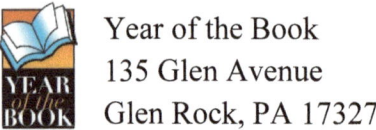 Year of the Book
135 Glen Avenue
Glen Rock, PA 17327

ISBN: 978-1-64649-377-7 (paperback)
ISBN: 978-1-64649-378-4 (ebook)

No part of this publication may be reproduced, distributed, or transmitted in any form or by any means, including photocopying, recording, or other electronic or mechanical methods, without the prior written permission of the publisher, except as permitted by U.S. copyright law.

Dedication

In memory of my three "moms"

Esther Hall Sanner, my gifted mother

Viola Hall Colflesh Bowser, my dearest aunt

Blanche Will Weaver, my sweet mother-in-law

Laughter is brightest where food is best.

– Irish proverb

Contents

The Gift Giver 1

Cranberries and Shopping Local 7

Embracing Traditions, Old and New 11

What's in a Name? 17

My Christmas Isn't Christmas Without Glazed Ham ... 23

Now We're Talking Turkey! 29

Christmas Dinner for Two 33

There Must Be Cookies! 39

Pumpkin Pie, a Necessity in My Family 45

Christmas Cookies and Memories 51

Christmas Cookie Tradition 57

Christmas Fudge, a Family Tradition 63

The Gift Giver

Christmas, for many, is a beautiful holiday filled with celebration, reverence, gift giving, and festive décor. At just the thought of Christmas, I am filled with a sense of awe and wonder, a childlike excitement and anticipation, and adoration and joy. I love the atmosphere, music, decorations, aromas, and sentiments.

There is one area, however, that I find a bit difficult about the holiday, and that's the aspect of gifts. Don't get me wrong, I love to give gifts. It's just that I'm not a good gift selector. There are a few people for whom I know immediately what is *exactly* the right thing. But for most of the gifts I want to give, I don't seem to be creative enough to come up with something I'm satisfied is suitable, one I hope will convey just how much the person means to me.

A dear friend, Kathleen Shoop, is the best gift giver I've ever known. She bestows presents throughout the year, always spot-on for the individual, and always unexpected, welcome, and appreciated. Her generosity and thoughtfulness seem to know no bounds. Kathie, as she is known by most of her friends and acquaintances, goes even further and exquisitely giftwraps each item in beautiful and unique ways.

In addition to her gift-giving expertise, I've never met anyone who is as enthralled with Christmas. At the mention of this holiday, Kathie's eyes actually twinkle, her face lights up, her mouth curves into the loveliest of smiles. She says she has always loved this holiday.

When she was a child, Kathie's parents made Christmas special. Her parents, who were teachers, saved up throughout the year so they could give Kathie and her siblings numerous gifts. They always decorated and enjoyed making the day and season bright. On Christmas Eve, they went out for a special dinner, something they didn't often do the rest of the year. And they went to church services where Kathie enjoyed the rituals and ceremony.

Her grandparents would come on Christmas Day, laden with huge bags of gifts. Both of Kathie's parents came from large families and she enjoyed all the time and celebration with relatives. She and her siblings got to help decorate, which Kathie loved doing. Her childhood holidays gave her the foundation upon which to create her own style of celebrations, combining tradition with new ideas.

In the early years of her marriage, Kathie and her husband hosted large and lovely Christmas Eve parties for family and friends. The house was lovingly decorated and menus planned to create a magical evening for the guests. But the highlight of the parties was that each year Kathie asked her guests to bring a coat to donate to the halfway house that was in her neighborhood. They would gather the coats, bundle them, and then place them on the front porch late that evening so the residents would find them the next morning, a Christmas surprise for those less fortunate.

Kathie and her husband took a short hiatus from the annual parties when their children were born, nearly a year apart, both preemies. But soon afterward, they resumed the Christmas Eve party tradition, with a twist—the celebrations also became a birthday party for their daughter who was born on December 25th, which Kathie says was her most magical Christmas.

As a prolific author, Kathie doesn't have a lot of time to cook, so she appreciates recipes that make enough for several meals. This tortellini soup is a dish she makes Christmas week that can be served as a starter for the Christmas feast as well as quick meals on busy days or lazy lunches leading up to and following Christmas Day. It's delicious, easy to make, and is a favorite for the Shoop family.

Enjoy the recipe, and I hope you look for some of Kathleen Shoop's books. She's written several lovely Christmas novellas as well as numerous historical fiction series. Her books are well researched and expertly written, and certainly enjoyable reading. If you find Christmas even just a portion as magical as Kathie does, it will be lovely indeed.

MERRY CHRISTMAS!

Kathie's Tortellini Soup

Ingredients

1 T butter
1/2 lg yellow or white onion, diced
3 small cloves garlic, minced
3 T tomato paste
1 tsp Italian seasoning
½ tsp red pepper flakes
3 T flour

3 c chicken broth
1 28-oz can diced tomatoes
4 c cheese tortellini
½ c freshly grated Parmesan
1/3 c cream
3 c fresh spinach, packed
2 T fresh basil, thinly sliced

Directions

1. In large pot over medium heat, melt butter. Add onions and cook until translucent, about 3 minutes. Add garlic and cook until fragrant, about 1 minute.

2. Add tomato paste, Italian seasoning, and red pepper flakes and cook, stirring, for one minute. Add flour and whisk to combine. Cook 1 more minute.

3. Add broth, tomatoes, and tortellini. Bring to a boil and then simmer until tortellini is cooked, about 10 minutes.

4. Add cream and Parmesan, stirring to combine. Add spinach and let wilt. Season with salt and pepper to taste. Garnish with basil and serve.

NOTE: Kathie sometimes uses canned tomatoes that already have Italian seasoning. If using these, omit or reduce the amount of dried seasoning.

Cranberries and Shopping Local

Cranberries are an important part of my winter holiday meals, both Thanksgiving and Christmas. I love the tart-sweet taste, and their vibrant color adds to the festive mood.

I find it a curiosity how traditions start or what causes us to select specific recipes for a given occasion. For me, I want homemade cranberry sauce for Thanksgiving dinner, but for Christmas, I prefer cranberry relish. That's not to say that I wouldn't gladly eat either one, but somehow, I developed this pattern.

If you've not made your own cranberry sauce or relish, I heartily encourage you to do so. It's so simple, and the taste is a world better than what you can purchase canned or premade at a supermarket. Not only do the sauce and relish make a lovely and delicious side dish but they are also good as a topping for a leftover turkey or ham sandwich, on top of stuffing, and even mixed in with your breakfast yogurt or oatmeal.

Buying fresh cranberries, along with the oranges for relish, as well as many other ingredients needed for Christmas dinner makes me think of the quaint and treasured fresh produce market in my hometown. Cascio's Fruit Market, a family-owned mainstay in Somerset, Pennsylvania, recently celebrated their 105th year in operation.

Not only have they been in business for that long, but also in the same building, which from the outside looks small, but once inside, shoppers are treated to an array of good foods and merchandise. While the name says "fruit market," they provide much more to their customer base—fresh vegetables, local honey and maple syrup, coffee, fresh baked breads and sweet treats, canned goods, dairy products, locally made jam and jelly, frozen seafood, fresh flowers, and even gift items. There are also ready-to-eat selections available including salads and sandwiches.

Their produce is especially delicious, high quality, and well-priced, and their customer service is unparalleled in our area. Late spring and summer months, much of the produce is locally grown. I particularly love their asparagus and sweet corn. The owners, Don and Jodi Brougher, are community-minded and help where and when they can. I love walking into the store, knowing that I'm going to get good products for a great price and with courteous staff to help me if needed.

I've come to rely on Cascio's for beautiful Christmas gift baskets and boxes which are bountifully filled with delicious products. Some of the baskets can be shipped across the country, and local baskets can be delivered by staff, if you like. Examples of the themed baskets include Italian Dinner and Pennsylvania, and the boxes feature Game Day, Somerset County, and more. Cascio's will even customize these for you.

Everyone I've sent these gifts to has been thoroughly impressed and pleased. It's so nice to have such a great market nearby, and one that has survived the ups and downs of business these many years. I'm sure their success is because of their desire to provide quality products at fair prices, and because they take pride in their role in our community. That's a Christmas gift in itself. Every small town should be as fortunate.

I hope you'll try this relish recipe. It couldn't be any simpler, and at the same time, yields a complex and delicious flavor.

MERRY CHRISTMAS!

Cranberry Relish

Ingredients

12-oz bag of fresh cranberries
1 orange, with peel on
1 c granulated sugar

Directions

1. Wash and dry the orange. Cut a very thin slice off the end of the orange. Leave the rest of the peel on the orange and slice the whole orange into 8 pieces.

2. Place the fresh cranberries, orange slices with peel, and sugar in the food processor and pulse until fairly smooth.

3. Refrigerate until ready to serve. Tastes best after chilling for an hour or more. Keeps for 1 week in refrigerator and can freeze up to 3 months. If frozen, allow to thaw in the refrigerator.

Embracing Traditions, Old and New

My childhood Christmas dinners were pretty standard fare without change. We always had turkey and all the trimmings, with an occasional year featuring a glazed ham. For my own family, however, I introduced a few different foods, primarily side dishes, while keeping most of what was traditional from my childhood, which I think is common practice for many families.

I was happy to try new things from my husband's family experience, with one exception. I admit I was obstinate. My sweet mother-in-law always served rigatoni with her Christmas ham dinner, and my husband loved the tradition. But for me, that just was not a good blend. I loved pasta, but I felt it had no place at Christmas. I don't know why, but the whole idea felt aversive to me. I was not going to ruin my Christmas dinners with rigatoni. That behavior was out of character for me, yet I just couldn't do it.

Then along came Christmas 2022. Everything was different. We were having Christmas in Florida, and the hopes of kids coming to join us were dashed late in the planning stages due to weather, bizarre airline issues, and concerns for health. So, the result was that we were having dinner for two, and I decided to be daring and really change it up. I went with steak au poivre instead of my usual ham. And since I felt like I was already going rogue, I acquiesced and surprised my husband with baked rigatoni to accompany our beef Christmas dinner.

Oh my goodness, my husband was so happy! And I felt guilty for not having taken his affection for his family tradition as seriously as I should have. To add to the surprise, I loved it too! Of course, I knew that many Italian families have various pasta dishes at Christmas, but not being Italian, it just didn't seem authentic for me to include it in my boring-ethnicity style dinner.

I've always loved to learn about dishes from other cultures and like to make many new-to-me foods. But I had this stumbling block when it came to changing up *my* family holiday traditions too much, especially in that way. I still don't understand why I was so stubborn about the inclusion of rigatoni.

I enjoyed learning about dishes my friend Wende Dikec eats at her family Christmas dinners. She has mixed Italian and Polish family ties with some French Canadian thrown in, too. Plus, her husband is originally from Turkey, and they met while living and working in Japan. She has interesting stories to tell! (Good thing she's a great writer and teacher.)

Wende and her immediate family typically go to visit her extended family for Christmas dinners. She takes along dishes that she prepares, and they enjoy the large family gatherings. These include Italian wedding soup and, for the Polish side of the family, pierogies. She recalls from childhood that her parents would go to a local mushroom farm where the mushrooms were grown in a cave to get fresh ones for the pierogies at Christmas Eve dinner.

Since Wende's husband Demir did not have Turkish foods or customs for Christmas, what they have done with their three sons is to hold a fancy meal for New Year's Eve to celebrate his heritage.

Wende also told me of an interesting custom she observed while living in Japan. While the Japanese did not celebrate the religious aspect of Christmas, they did decorate and on Christmas Eve would have special date nights for couples. On this date, it was customary for the woman to give the man chocolates.

I find it fascinating to learn of traditions and customs of other cultures and ethnicities. Now, after my Christmas 2022 alterations to my old standards, things will be changing with future holiday meals and developing new legacies. I hope you, too, will enjoy elements of your past and combine them with new additions.

ENJOY!

Baked Rigatoni

Ingredients

1 T olive oil
1 lb ground beef
1 lb mild Italian sausage, casings removed
1/2 c finely chopped onion
2 small cloves garlic, minced
24-oz jar marinara sauce
8 oz can tomato sauce
2 tsp Italian seasoning
salt and pepper to taste
1 lb rigatoni pasta, cooked acc. to package directions
2 c shredded mozzarella
2 T chopped parsley

Directions

1. Heat oil in large pan over medium high heat. Add the ground beef and sausage. Season with salt and pepper. Cook until starting to brown, breaking meat into small pieces. Add onion and continue cooking until meat is cooked through and onions are softened.

2. Add garlic and cook for 30 seconds. Add the marinara, tomato sauce, and Italian seasoning to the pan and bring to simmer. Allow the sauce to simmer for 10 minutes.

3. Preheat oven to 350 degrees. Grease a 9x13 dish.

4. Combine the cooked rigatoni with the sauce. Pour into greased dish and top with mozzarella. Cover with foil and bake for 20 minutes, then uncover and bake for another 15-20 minutes or until pasta is bubbly and cheese is melted and browned.

5. Remove from oven and sprinkle with parsley. Let stand for 5 minutes, then serve.

What's in a Name?

What do you call that bowl of herby goodness chockful of butter, celery, onions, sage, and parsley? Is it "stuffing" or "dressing" or perhaps even known as "filling"? All are names for a flavorful dish, typically bread-based, that exudes the quintessential aromas of a holiday meal. Regional and ethnic differences as well as family traditions and personal preferences seem to dictate the choice of ingredients and method of preparation.

I grew up with all three names referring to the same dish. For some reason my mom used the terms interchangeably. As a young adult I heard others sticking to just one term and I wanted to know if there was a difference. Most sources explained stuffing and dressing as being the same mixture, with stuffing cooked inside a turkey or other poultry while dressing was baked in a dish. Filling typically referred to a Pennsylvania Dutch dish that used mashed potatoes as the main ingredient, usually supplemented with bread and always baked separate from the bird.

My later research led me to a wider variety of forms and preferences. While some people do still expressly differentiate stuffing from dressing, many do not make that distinction. For example, in the southern United States, dressing is used for either type of preparation. Some northerners call their casserole dish stuffing even though it didn't go near a turkey, chicken, or meat. I don't believe it is common for anyone to call their form of stuffing or dressing by the Pennsylvania Dutch name of filling unless it truly is filling, that is, made with mashed potatoes.

It seems that cooks originated stuffing primarily from items readily available, and often as a way to use up stale bread or other ingredients, not wanting them to go to waste. While I was accustomed to white bread used for stuffing, some people use cornbread, and in the Great Lakes area, many use wild rice.

Most dressing recipes include bread, celery, onion, butter, and maybe eggs, plus sage and parsley. A variety of additions are not uncommon, such as giblets, sausage, cranberries, oysters, or nuts, depending on preferences. It was once thought that the use of oysters was limited to coastal areas, but the practice continued in the middle of the country also, with transplants wanting a touch of home as well as featuring something really special for a holiday meal. I had always assumed cornbread's use in dressing was strictly a southern practice, but it turns out it's also used in other parts of the country.

Yet another version exists—stuffing balls. I was first introduced to this delectable dish by my college roommate. After going home to Elkins, West Virginia, for an occasional weekend, Ellen always brought her mother's delicious stuffing balls back to campus for a treat and generously shared with me. Many years went by until I was once again reminded of stuffing balls, this time from a childhood friend, Melba (Mel) Campbell Drenning.

Mel and I met in grade school at Kingwood Elementary, part of the Rockwood School District. We lost touch after high school, but a few years ago reconnected. Mel lives in Idaho and recently shared a photo on social media showing trays of stuffing balls she'd made for her family. The photo was tantalizing and sparked my interest in making them myself.

Like many great cooks, Mel doesn't use a recipe, but did share some tips with me. She cooks onions and celery in "lots" of butter, adding that to bread cubes. She then beats together eggs, salt, pepper, sage, and poultry seasoning, adding some broth if needed to moisten the bread. After forming balls, she pours chicken stock around them in the pan and covers with foil to bake. She prefers having the tops "crusted" so she removes the foil for the last part of baking.

Stuffing, in whatever form you prefer, need not be reserved only for a Thanksgiving turkey. It tastes great with roast beef or chicken, for stuffed pork chops, or as a side dish with ham. It has a presence on my Christmas dinner menu, no matter what meat or poultry I am serving. This recipe is a combination of my traditional stuffing recipe, others that I found, and incorporates my friend Mel's suggestions. I hope you enjoy these as much as I do.

MERRY CHRISTMAS!

Stuffing & Stuffing Balls

Ingredients

Lg loaf bread, several days old
   (approx. 16 c cubes)
3/4 c unsalted butter
1 med onion, chopped
   (white or yellow)
3-4 stalks celery, chopped
4 eggs
2 tsp poultry seasoning
1 tsp dry rubbed sage
2 heaping T dried parsley
1 tsp salt
1/4 tsp ground black pepper
Approx. 1 c chicken or turkey
   stock

Directions

1. Tear or cut bread into approx. 1-1/2 inch pieces and spread on cookie tray to dry for an hour or two, tossing the bread cubes a few times.

2. In saucepan, melt butter, then add onion and celery, cooking over medium heat until soft, about 15 minutes. Let cool for 10 minutes.

3. Put bread into large bowl. Add celery mixture, and toss together.

4. In medium bowl, beat eggs together. Add herbs and spices and about 1/4 cup stock.

5. Add egg mixture to bread cubes and mix together. If needed, add a little extra stock.

6. Scoop stuffing into balls (ice cream scoop works well). Slightly press each ball to help it keep its shape. Place balls in casserole dish.

7. Carefully pour stock around the balls to about 1/4-inch depth. Cover with foil and bake in 350-degree oven for 20 minutes. Remove foil and bake an additional 10-15 minutes until lightly browned and slightly crisp on top. (Makes 12 baseball-sized balls.)

NOTE: Stuffing balls can be frozen before or after baking. Recipe can easily be doubled.

My Christmas Isn't Quite Christmas without Glazed Ham

The holidays are here, and Christmas is the shining star. Such a magical, reverent, and joyous time that is filled with hope for many. This most special holiday season of festivities and splendid decorations readily lends well to celebratory meals with family and dear friends.

At the top of my dinner list is the Christmas ham, although it has not always been a tradition in my family. As I was growing up, sometimes we did have ham, but more often turkey was featured. I'm not sure what factors were involved in my mother's decision, but ham was definitely my favorite. I recall that she decorated the ham with clove-studded pineapple rings and maraschino cherries. It was pretty as well as delicious.

One long-standing tradition that my mother started for our family was serving Christmas dinner on Christmas Eve. I've always enjoyed that and have continued the practice. I love having leftovers on Christmas Day, making it a leisurely way to spend time with family instead of being in the kitchen.

For the many years that I have prepared Christmas meals, I've included ham, even if a different item was the star feature of the meal. At times I've made Cornish game hens, frequently a turkey, but always include a baked glazed ham. I know some families prefer a Christmas goose or a nice Beef Wellington, or a rib roast with Yorkshire pudding. Others may serve a rack of lamb, pheasant, roast pork, or a seafood dish. For me, however, it isn't quite Christmas dinner without the pineapple-glazed smoked ham that I find so tantalizing.

Ham is a cured back leg of pork. Country or fresh ham is uncooked, while what we typically find in the supermarket is a "city" ham, one that is fully cooked. The tradition of eating ham at Christmas harkens back to the Yule ham, which began first as an old custom dating to the pre-Christian era when Germanic tribes sacrificed wild boars to a Norse god.

There are several options available today when choosing your ham: bone-in, boneless, spiral-cut, smoked, and fresh. I much prefer bone-in or semi-boneless, finding these to be moister, more tender, and with better flavor. My experience is that boneless hams tend to dry out quickly and are not as flavorful. I've recently read that baking spiral-cut hams in an oven-proof plastic bag helps to prevent dryness, but I have not yet tried that.

Sometimes I bake my ham in two pieces, one to glaze, the other to keep plain to later incorporate in dishes where I would not want a sweet taste. Some of my favorites are scalloped potatoes, bean soup, omelets, and ham salad. I've only recently come to enjoy ham potpie.

I love to see the table set for Christmas dinner, whatever meat is center stage, with candles and festive linens. It adds to the mood and memories, making the meal that extra special event that is well worth the effort.

I hope you enjoy this recipe for pineapple-glazed baked ham.

MERRY CHRISTMAS!

Pineapple-Glazed Baked Ham

Ingredients

Semi-boneless smoked ham (or your favorite)
1 c brown sugar, packed
1 T plus 1 tsp cornstarch
1/4 tsp salt
Pinch of ground cloves
1 small can (8-1/2 oz) crushed pineapple in syrup
2 T fresh lemon juice
1 T prepared yellow mustard

Directions

1. Place ham in roasting pan and add enough water to cover bottom of pan, about 1/4-inch deep. Cover loosely with lid or foil. Bake at 325 degrees for 15 minutes per pound.

2. As ham bakes, stir brown sugar, cornstarch, ground cloves, and salt together in saucepan. Add pineapple, with syrup, lemon juice, and mustard. Mix well and cook over medium heat to a slow boil, stirring constantly, until thickens into a glaze. (Color will darken to a light caramel.)

3. Take ham out of oven about 30 minutes before done; remove pan drippings, then spoon glaze over the ham and return to oven for 30 minutes. Reserve 3/4 cup of glaze to serve alongside ham, if you wish.

4. Let rest for about 15 minutes before carving.

NOTE: If using a whole ham, double this recipe.

❧ Now We're Talking Turkey! ❧

As I was growing up, our Christmas meal was much alike the iconic Thanksgiving dinner: roast turkey, stuffing, gravy, mashed potatoes, homemade noodles, candied yams, peas, corn, cranberry sauce, and dinner rolls. The savory scents of sage, thyme, parsley, celery, and onion beckoned the entire family. Creamy pumpkin pie, just sweet enough, always topped off the meal. Occasionally Mom would make a baked ham instead of turkey and still served many of the same side dishes.

We always had our dinner on Christmas Eve, and the leftovers on Christmas Day were nearly as highly prized as the hot, freshly prepared star itself. Cold turkey sandwiches with either mustard or mayonnaise, and cranberry sauce as a side made a great lunch. And for dinner, the turkey and all the accompaniments were reheated for another sumptuous meal. I especially loved leftover stuffing with gravy; I salivate just thinking of it!

My parents were both hard workers and didn't often take time off. My dad, a small-business owner, labored seven days a week for the bulk of his working life. So, for both of them, Christmas Day was their primary day to relax out of the whole year. That's why a Christmas Eve dinner appealed so much to my mom. Turkey leftovers on Christmas Day were perfect. She could sit back and relax, enjoy the revelry of kids opening gifts, and not fuss with a big dinner to prepare.

Interestingly, the United States is one of the top producers for turkeys. In addition to preparing the traditional stuffed and roasted bird, some people enjoy deep fried, barbequed, brined, or smoked turkey. According to the Oxford Companion to American Food and Drink, Amelia Simmons, the first American to publish a cookbook, included five turkey recipes in her *American Cookery*, published way back in 1796.

The same reference book explains that turkeys found in the Americas were introduced to the Caribbean islands by 1520, and to Spain shortly after. Turkey proved to be a good food source and spread throughout Europe. When British colonists arrived in America, they were already familiar with turkey as a diet staple.

No matter how much one likes turkey, most likely you'll be looking for ways to use up the extra meat. Pot pie is delicious and a good way to also incorporate vegetables you may have. My mother made excellent pot pies, the type using piecrust filled with a mixture of meat and vegetables in thick gravy. She often froze them, which made a great meal when she was short on time. It's probably my favorite use of poultry leftovers. I also enjoy beef pot pie.

In whatever way you celebrate the holiday, I wish you a Merry Christmas, filled with love, warmth, and good food.

Turkey Pot Pie

Ingredients

2 round piecrusts
   (homemade or purchased)
3 c* cooked turkey
2 T butter
1/2 small onion, chopped
1 celery stalk, chopped
1 russet potato, peeled,
   cubed and cooked

2 c* assorted cooked veggies
   (carrots, peas, corn, beans)
2 c** turkey gravy
1/4 tsp dried sage, ground
1/4 tsp thyme, crushed
1 tsp dried parsley

Directions

1. Melt butter in saucepan. Add onion and celery, sautéeing until nearly tender.

2. Carefully pour in turkey gravy and simmer over low heat until warm.

3. Combine enough gravy with turkey and assorted vegetables to the thickness you like.

4. Place one piecrust round in a 9-inch pie plate. Allow turkey mixture to cool a little, then pour into plate. Top with second piecrust, crimping edges well to prevent overflow.

6. Cut several slits in top piecrust to allow steam to escape.

6. Bake at 425 for 15 minutes, then lower oven to 350 degrees and bake for an additional 35 minutes or until crust is browned to your liking.

Tips

Brushing the top crust just before baking with either a small amount of milk or beaten egg helps the crust brown to a nice golden color.

*Adjust amounts of turkey and vegetables according to your preferences and what you have available.

**If you don't have leftover gravy, make a traditional white sauce with equal parts butter and flour cooked together, then add equal parts chicken broth and milk. Cook mixture until thickened. Add salt and pepper to taste.

Christmas Dinner for Two

I thoroughly enjoy the coziness of settling in for the approaching winter, baking and cooking for the holiday, eager for special time to visit with family and friends, and the exultant sounds of Christmas music, both sacred and secular. The beautiful sensory details that fill the air throughout the season are mesmerizing and tantalizing.

My memories of Christmas as a child are flooded with shiny reds, greens, golds, and silvers, from decorations to gift packages. My exquisitely artistic mother was skilled at decorating our home, and she loved turning our Christmas tree into a work of art, making it a showpiece. Her gift-wrapping was a close second as she tenderly crafted bows and placed them "just so" on each meticulously tagged and color-coordinated package.

The week between Christmas and New Year's Day was a fun-filled time with visiting grandparents and aunts and cousins, "seeing what Santa brought" each year, and excited oohs and aahs. There were cookies and pies, candy canes and chocolate-covered cherries, hot chocolate and eggnog devoured and quaffed by all.

I miss the beauty of my childhood Christmases, with my mother's beautiful trees and detailed decorating throughout the house, but there are always new opportunities and adventures waiting to be discovered that can shape one's view. I love to entertain and cook for family and guests, usually the more the merrier. And for Christmas, we love having as many family members visiting as possible.

However, during the pandemic and subsequent years, our family gatherings had to change out of necessity. My husband and I came to realize, and at first only reluctantly accepting, our Christmas dinner was going to include only the two of us, a major change. So no more lavish table spread with numerous dishes accompanied by lots of laughter and conversation followed by games and more laughter.

I had to revamp my approach for creating the special holiday meal, and while I missed what had been, I was determined to embrace this new plan for what it was, and accept that life brings changes and challenges, and it's up to each of us to try to make the best of things. We could adapt and adjust.

So, Christmas dinner for two was on the menu for the last three years, and while we missed having the kids home, we embraced technology and had group Zoom visits, redirected some of the gift giving to the form of charitable donations, and counted ourselves fortunate for so many wonderful years of large family gatherings.

The first two years, I attempted to keep the holiday meal similar to past celebrations while adapting size and quantity. Last year I decided to venture into new territory and make a delicious beef dish, Steak au Poivre, instead. It seemed perfect for Christmas dinner for two, and although easy to make, it is an elegant dish.

A French-named dish meaning "pepper steak," it is a good quality beef steak coated in crushed peppercorns, seared, and served with a flavored cream sauce. There are many claims as to who first created the dish. A chef at the Restaurant Albert on the Champs-Elysees in Paris claimed to have created it in 1930. Another chef, M. Deveaux, claimed the honor at Maxim's in 1920. However, others state it was in existence in Monte Carlo in 1910, while another chef, O. Becker, insisted that he was preparing the dish as early as 1905 at the once-famous Parisian restaurant Paillard's.

No matter who truly came up with the idea first, the result is a tender, tasty entrée that is easier to make than one might think, and yet sure to please your family or guests. The key to this fabulous steak is the peppercorns, a berry-like fruit of the pepper plant. We all have grown accustomed to black pepper as a common seasoning, an almost certain partner to salt in most savory recipes.

Over the centuries, pepper has played a significant role both for seasoning food, as well as in commerce. In the 1500s, there was great economic competition over pepper between Portugal, the English, and the Dutch. The United States entered the global pepper trade in the 1790s. A sea captain from Salem, Massachusetts, sailed to the East Indies, acquired peppercorns, was shipwrecked off Bermuda, then found his way home again, and eventually sold his load of pepper at a 700 percent profit.

Black pepper is believed to have originated on the Malabar Coast of India. The pepper vines bear white flowers that appear like berries and become peppercorns. They ripen from green to red to brown, and the stage at which they are harvested determines the type of pepper. The black pepper we typically consume is harvested from dried red peppercorns. Other types of pepper are white and green.

I hope you try this recipe. It really is easy to prepare yet impressive for entertaining and makes a lovely Christmas dinner for two. I used beef filet, but a good quality steak such as ribeye works as well. Pear, peach, or apricot juices are good non-alcoholic substitutes for cognac if you desire. You may want to adjust the amount of peppercorns to suit your tastes and tolerance to heat from the pepper.

Here's to a wonderful Christmas dinner, no matter the number of people sitting around your table.

ENJOY!

Steak au Poivre

Ingredients

Approx. 1 lb beef filets
  about 1-1/4 in thick
  (or tenderloin, boneless
  ribeye, strip steak)
Kosher salt
1 T whole peppercorns
  (use more or less according
  to tolerance and preference)

1 T olive oil
1 T unsalted butter, divided
1/2 med shallot, finely chopped
6 T plus 1 tsp cognac
  (or brandy)
Scant cup of heavy cream

Directions

1. Set out steaks at room temperature for 30 minutes.

2. Crack peppercorns using mortar and pestle, or place in plastic bag and pound with rolling pin or meat mallet. Place cracked pepper on a plate.

3. Pat steaks dry and season with Kosher salt, then dredge in cracked peppercorns, pressing lightly to adhere pepper to steak.

4. Heat olive oil and half the butter in heavy skillet over medium to medium-high heat. When oil is shimmering, gently place steaks in skillet and cook 4-5 minutes each side, turning only once. After cooking both sides, remove steaks to plate and tent with foil.

5. Carefully pour off any excess grease, allowing a small amount to remain in skillet. Add remaining butter to skillet and place over medium heat. Sauté shallots until soft while scraping the skillet, about 2 minutes.

6. Turn off the heat. Carefully pour in the 6 T cognac. Turn heat back on immediately to medium and bring to boil while continuing to scrape the brown bits from bottom of skillet. Cook for several minutes until the cognac is mostly evaporated and a slight glaze forms.

7. Pour in the heavy cream and boil while whisking for about 5 minutes until sauce is velvety and slightly thickened. Add 1 tsp cognac and salt to taste. Return steaks to pan, including any juices that have collected. Spoon sauce over steaks and serve. (Makes 3-4 servings.)

There Must be Cookies!

In my family, as it is for many, December means Christmas is coming and it's time for some serious cookie baking. Added to glowing Christmas lights, melodic tones of carols, and the scent of evergreen branches, the aroma and taste of freshly baked cookies evoke nostalgic and happy memories.

My mother-in-law, Blanche Weaver, was a great cookie baker, and going to her house at Christmas meant lots and lots of cookies. Similar to my house, but with one difference—she always made the same kind of cookies each year, at least as long as I knew her, and without those repeat appearances, the grandchildren and her grown kids would have been devastated.

A sweet, kind, and unassuming woman, Blanche stressed fairness and doted on her three kids and their families. To get to her living room, everyone had to pass through her kitchen where, on Christmas Day, countertops were lined with trays of cookies. The usual suspects: black & white cheesecake bars, sand tarts, lemon bars, sugar cookies, and chocolate chip cookies.

Her three adult children as well as the grandkids grabbed cookies as they passed through on the way to the living room for gift opening. More cookies were consumed as gifts were exchanged, and dinner was served with everyone continuing to stuff themselves with cookies even while consuming the "real food" of Christmas dinner. Then they had cookies along with their dessert of pie and ice cream. My husband may say that I'm exaggerating, but I am not. They are true cookie monsters!

Another important element of the holiday celebration that must be mentioned is leaving cookies for Santa! We always knew in our household that Santa's favorite kind was chocolate chip. We sometimes added pumpkin cookies as an extra treat, plus a few festively decorated sugar cookies cut into reindeer shapes.

Typically, I find it easier to work alone in the kitchen. However, Christmas cookie baking was always a fun project with the kids when they were young. When my husband and I became empty-nesters, the cookie baking was not as much fun.

Enter a different type of recipe: Add several friends, stir, mix, and develop a new tradition. Several years ago, a few friends and I decided to get together to make Christmas cookies. Having the largest kitchen, I hosted. We each contributed our recipes and most of the ingredients. I had extra of the basics on hand, so we were in good shape.

We started about 9:00 in the morning, broke for a lunch of soup that I'd prepared in advance, and went back to baking until almost 5:00 P.M. It was a long day and we were tired, but oh so productive! Hundreds and hundreds of cookies of many shapes, sizes, flavors, and styles. A successful and rewarding day, we repeated it again and hope to continue the recent custom.

As we baked, we also talked, laughed, cried, and bolstered our friendship. When all the cookies were baked, we divvied up the wares, each taking home dozens of each type of cookie, plus more that we donated to our church's annual Christmas musical. Performed by the children and youth of St. Paul's UCC in Somerset, PA, and directed by Marcy Shellenberger-Steinly, the musical, too, is a highlight of our holiday celebrations.

I'm sharing Blanche's Black & White Cheesecake Bars recipe. It is easy and delicious, and I hope you enjoy adding it to your holiday preparations.

MERRY CHRISTMAS!

Blanche's Cheesecake Bars

Ingredients

1 (12 oz.) pkg. semi-sweet chocolate chips
1/2 c butter
2 c graham cracker crumbs
1 (8 oz.) pkg. cream cheese
1 (14 oz.) can sweetened condensed milk
1 egg
1 tsp vanilla

Directions

1. In medium saucepan over low heat, melt chocolate chips and butter, stirring until smooth. Remove from heat.

2. Stir in graham cracker crumbs. Reserve 1/4 cup mixture for topping. Press the remaining mixture in 9x13 baking pan.

3. In large bowl, beat cream cheese with electric mixer until smooth. Gradually beat in sweetened condensed milk, then egg and vanilla.

4. Pour over prepared crust. Sprinkle with 1/4 cup reserved crumb mixture.

5. Bake in 325 degree oven until set, 25-30 minutes. Cool. Refrigerate about 2 hours. Cut into squares. (Yield: 35 squares)

Refrigerate leftover cookies.

Pumpkin Pie, A Necessity in My Family

Pumpkin, the perennial harbinger of fall and the holiday season, is delicious in many foods including the iconic pumpkin pie and sweet treats like cookies, muffins, breads, bars, and lovely cream-cheese frosting-filled pumpkin roll. It also works well in savory dishes such as pumpkin soup, curry, fritters, risotto, and gnocchi. The seeds and blossoms are edible as well, and pumpkin has even become popular in flavoring craft beers.

Thought to have originated about 5500 B.C. in Central America, pumpkins are of mainly two types: the smaller pie pumpkin, also known as sugar or sweet, and the larger Jack-o'-lantern type, sometimes called field pumpkins, meant for carving and decorating. The large field varieties can be cooked and eaten, but they are less sweet and have less "meat" to them. The earliest pumpkin pies were basically hollowed out pumpkins filled with milk and then roasted.

I like to use fresh pumpkin for savory dishes but prefer the consistency and deep flavor of canned pumpkin for pie and other baked goods. Fresh is quite watery and requires repeated draining; they are easy to prepare otherwise. Simply cut in half, scrape out the seeds and pulp, and roast in oven on a tray, or cook in a slow cooker. When soft, let cool until easy to handle and scrape out the flesh. Process through a food mill and drain several times.

Tied with black raspberry as my favorite pie, with a few close seconds, the custardy spice-filled pumpkin pie is almost a ritual. I *must* have pumpkin pie for breakfast on both Thanksgiving and Christmas mornings. And so do the kids. It's definitely a family tradition.

Pumpkin pie for breakfast stemmed from my childhood, placing such high importance on what, to me, was a delicacy, that I had to consume as much as possible during those two important holidays, and the only time out of the year when my mother made pumpkin pies. I guess I was a bit greedy, but I needed to fill that void of deprivation having gone most of the year without this scrumptious treat.

However, there is sound reasoning to have pumpkin pie for breakfast. It is chockful of eggs and milk, both great protein sources, and with the additional benefits of beta-carotene, vitamins, and fiber from the pumpkin which all point to a good and relatively healthy breakfast dish, especially if you reduce the sugar in the recipe. I've been known to bake the custard portion in a pie plate, without crust, to save calories. I wouldn't do this for holidays, but for an average day treat, it's perfect.

I hope you try my recipe; my family says it's the best. I believe the key to a perfect pumpkin pie is using canned pumpkin puree (not pie filling!) and to be certain it's baked long enough that the flavors truly meld and deepen. Enjoy, and don't forget to have some for Christmas morning's breakfast.

MomDoodle's Best Pumpkin Pie

Ingredients

1 can (29 oz.) pure pumpkin puree
3/4 c granulated sugar
3/4 c packed brown sugar
1 tsp salt
2 tsp ground cinnamon
1 tsp ground ginger
1/2 tsp ground cloves
1/8 tsp ground nutmeg
1/8 tsp allspice
2 tsp vanilla extract
4 eggs
2 cans (12 oz. each) evaporated milk
2 unbaked pie crusts

Directions

1. Using a whisk, thoroughly mix pumpkin, sugar, salt, spices, and vanilla.

2. Whisk in eggs, one at a time.

3. Add the canned milk gradually, mixing thoroughly.

4. Pour into unbaked pie crust and bake at 450 degrees for 12 minutes, then reduce temperature to 350 degrees and bake until knife inserted in center comes out clean and custard has developed a deep color, about 50-60 minutes. (If edges of crust are getting too brown, carefully place a ring of foil around the crust rim.)

NOTE: Best results with Libby brand pumpkin and Carnation evaporated milk.

Christmas Cookies and Memories

Ah, the sweet and spicy aromas of cinnamon, brown sugar, ginger, nutmeg, molasses, and more fill the air in our homes this month. December is such a heartwarming and body warming time with cooking and baking for the holidays.

I think many of us relish preparing and sharing gifts, treats, and meals from our kitchens. Whether baking cookies, making candy, toasting spiced nuts, or creating jarred soup mixes, it's a lovely and rewarding activity to share love through the foods we prepare.

One of my favorite Christmas memories was going to my grandmother's house. Grandma had been widowed long before I was born, and she struggled financially. But her house was always the gathering place for her six daughters and their children. It just occurred to me as I write this that the spouses did not typically visit. I don't know why I'd never noticed that before. I guess the men didn't care to join all the ladies and children crammed into a small house.

But Grandma's "girls" brought plenty of food with them, trays of cookies and other treats, sandwiches, ice cream, and probably covered dishes, but I mostly remember the desserts. We had such fun with lots of cousins to play with and share new toys and gifts. There's no one food item that stands out in my memory, just a great time visiting, playing, and eating, and there was always music.

Baking and sharing Christmas cookies is a long-lived tradition that seems to make the holiday brighter and gives both the giver and recipient a special feeling of love and joy. My mother-in-law reigned supreme in the Christmas cookie realm, making a large variety and every one was delicious.

My mother baked cookies for the holidays as well, but certainly fewer in number and types. Her standard fare included the family favorite chocolate chip cookies as well as peanut butter and some years she made raisin filled cookies. There were always cut-out sugar cookies to decorate, although they were the last to be eaten.

One special variety that she made only at Christmas was what she called a nut cookie. As children, my brother and I joked that they looked like shrimp. However, I don't know why we even thought of that, as to the best of my knowledge, there had never been a single shrimp served in our home. However, the cookies came to be called shrimp cookies in our household and we kept the name into adulthood.

The cookies have a soft and just ever so subtle sweetness to the dough. They are filled with sweetened ground walnuts, rolled, and shaped into a crescent, then sprinkled with a touch of granulated sugar prior to baking. Over the years I have seen almost identical recipes called nut roll cookies as well as nut horns. There's also a similar looking cookie called a walnut crescent, but that has walnuts distributed throughout the cookie dough rather than being a filled cookie as my mother made them.

Supposedly, mom's recipe makes cookies that keep well. However, the cookies were so good, the supply never lasted long enough to test that theory. Mom only made them using walnuts, so I have not swayed from that practice and therefore cannot say if another type of nut would work. I hope you make and enjoy these delicious, shrimp-shaped nut cookies.

MERRY CHRISTMAS!

Mom's Favorite Nut ~shrimp~ Cookies

Dough
1 c butter
1 8-oz. pkg. Philly cream cheese
2-1/4 c flour

Filling
2 c ground walnuts (1/2 lb nuts)
1/2 c granulated sugar
1/4 - 1/2 c milk, scalded

Additional granulated sugar for rolling
Powdered sugar for coating

Directions

1. Beat cream cheese and butter together until light and creamy, about 5 minutes.

2. In separate bowl, sift together flour and salt. Add in small increments to the butter and cheese mixture, mixing well. Dough should be soft.

3. Divide dough into four portions, flatten into a disk, and wrap in plastic wrap. Refrigerate several hours until firm, or overnight.

4. Make filling by stirring together the nuts and sugar, then slowing adding milk until a nice spreading consistency. You may not need all the milk.

5. Roll out dough, one disk at a time, using additional granulated sugar on rolling surface. Pat a little flour on both sides of disk before rolling. Roll to a little under 1/8-inch thickness.

6. Cut out circles using 2-inch round cutter. Place a heaping 1/2 teaspoon of walnut mixture just off-center of each circle. Roll up, pinching to create a seam to keep filling inside, and dip top of cookie in granulated sugar. Shape into a crescent and place on baking tray with parchment paper.

7. Bake in preheated oven at 375 degrees on top rack for 12-14 minutes or until lightly browned on bottom. (The bottom browns much faster than top.) Repeat with remaining dough. Dough scraps can be rerolled after chilling again. Dust cookies with powdered sugar once completely cooled.

NOTE: If refrigerated dough is too firm, allow to rest at room temperature until easy to roll.

Christmas Cookie Tradition

They're almost synonymous—Christmas and cookies. The enjoyment (or chore, depending on your perspective) of baking dozens and dozens of at least several varieties; packaging to give as gifts; sharing when friends and family stop by; and of course, thoroughly enjoying many morsels with your cup of tea, coffee, or hot chocolate are all part of the magic of Christmas cookies.

I think for many children looking forward to Christmas morning, one of the most anticipated and exciting preludes is setting out cookies for Santa. Some families also leave carrots or special cookies for the reindeer. It's a fond memory for many of us.

It is thought that the tradition of leaving cookies and milk for Santa Claus took off in the United States during the 1930s as a result of the Great Depression. Parents wanted their children to learn the importance of giving to others and sharing, and that they should be thankful for the gifts they were fortunate enough to receive during those hard economic times.

The basis of this practice can be traced back to ancient Norse mythology. The god Odin was believed to have an eight-legged horse; children would put out food for the horse in hopes that during his travels, Odin would stop, allow his horse to eat, and would then leave gifts for the children in return.

Today, the custom takes various forms throughout the world. In Denmark, children still believe that horses lead Santa's sleigh, so they leave carrots and hay. In Great Britain and Australia, they put out mince pies for Santa. I guess it's not surprising that my Irish kin include a pint of Guinness along with their cookies to quench hard-working Santa's thirst.

I was surprised to learn that my British friend Hilary Hauck, a wonderful writer, did not have Christmas cookies as she was growing up. During her childhood living near London, family, friends, and neighbors instead had Christmas cakes and puddings; there were never any cookies, or biscuits as they call them, for Christmas.

Hilary's favorite dessert during her London years was the Christmas pudding her mother made. It had a very moist cake-like base with dried fruits topped by some brandy which her mother lit when she brought it to the table. Then each piece was drizzled with brandy butter. The top was decorated with a sprig of fresh holly, and inside the dessert, her mother hid a sixpence coin wrapped in foil. Whoever found the coin in their serving of pudding received good luck.

Hilary makes up for her previous lack of Christmas cookies now that she lives in the States. She enjoyed making and decorating cookies with her children and is carrying on that tradition with her grandchildren whom she calls her "grandorables." Christmas cookies figure into one of her Christmas novellas.

Here in the U.S., varieties of Christmas cookies can vary from the simple sugar cookie to something much more labor intensive such as making a proper French macaron, and those beautiful but time-consuming elaborately decorated cookies that grace many holiday cookie trays. Flavors can range from the very mild shortbread to an intense spicy-hot ginger cookie.

The whole process of cookie baking evokes many pleasures for me: reliving the memories of baking with my kids when they were young, absorbing the scents and textures of combining and baking the ingredients, experiencing the joy of sharing the tasty treats with friends, family, and people I may not even know.

I'm sharing a recipe for a favorite of mine that appears on my cookie trays every year. I often receive requests for the recipe. It's a drop cookie, which is easier, I think, than making shaped or pressed cookies. In addition to their delicious taste, the recipe for these pumpkin cookies makes a large batch and they freeze well. The recipe is flexible with various options for add-ins, with or without frosting.

Don't forget Santa's milk and cookies, plus carrots for the reindeer.

MERRY CHRISTMAS!

Pumpkin Drop Cookies

Ingredients

4 c all-purpose flour
2 tsp baking powder
2 tsp baking soda
1 tsp salt
1 tsp cinnamon
1/2 tsp nutmeg
1/8 tsp cloves
2 c granulated sugar
2 c butter, softened
2 eggs
2 tsp vanilla
1 (15-oz) canned pumpkin

Optional add-ins: mini chocolate chips, raisins, Craisins, nuts, coconut, butterscotch chips

Directions

1. In large bowl, combine flour, baking powder, baking soda, salt, and spices. Use a whisk to mix well. Set aside.

2. In large mixing bowl, combine sugar and butter and beat for several minutes until light and fluffy.

3. Add eggs, one at a time, completely blending in first egg before adding the second.

4. Add pumpkin puree and vanilla. Mix well.

5. Add flour mixture and mix until incorporated. You may need to finish mixing with a large wooden spoon if the mixer is getting bogged down.

6. If using a variety of add-ins, divide cookie dough into several smaller bowls and add desired extras.

7. Drop cookie dough onto ungreased or parchment-lined cookie sheets and bake at 375 degrees until top is set, and bottom just slightly starts to brown, approximately 10-15 minutes, depending on size of cookies.

8. Remove from oven and let cool 1 minute before transferring cookies to wire rack to finish cooling. Frost with brown sugar icing or cream cheese frosting, if desired.

Optional Maple-Brown Sugar Icing: Mix 1/2 cup packed brown sugar with 1/2 unsalted butter in small saucepan until butter melts and mixture is smooth and just beginning to bubble at edges. Cool completely. Then add 1/4 cup milk, 1 tsp maple flavoring, a pinch of salt, and 2-1/2 to 3 cups powdered sugar. Add a little more milk if too thick or add a little more powdered sugar if too thin. Mix well and top cookies. Sprinkle with finely chopped nuts.

Christmas Fudge, A Family Tradition

My favorite Christmas treat was my mother's peanut butter marshmallow fudge. My paternal grandmother's chocolate fudge was a close second. For the holiday, we baked tasty cookies and purchased popcorn balls, candy canes, chocolate-covered cherries, and Russell Stover's boxed chocolates. However, the homemade fudge was definitely the highlight of holiday treats.

I don't recall what my grandmother's cooking was like; I only remember her delicious, yeasty homemade bread with home-churned butter, no-bake cookies, and her chocolate fudge. She had a propensity for sweets and her housedress pockets always carried some treat, usually pink lozenges and butterscotch candies. In the family room, candy dishes typically held caramel creams, root beer barrels, circus peanuts, and spearmint gumdrops.

At Christmas, additional candy dishes were present, abundantly filled with ribbon candy, crème-filled chocolate drops, and peppermint straws. She shared gift tins of filled, hard tack candies; I always ate the raspberry and peanut butter ones first. The best, however, was when Grandma brought out the plates of her homemade chocolate fudge laden with walnuts. Now it was Christmas!

Alas, I don't have my grandmother's actual recipe, but I know she called it Million Dollar Fudge. Numerous recipes exist with that name, and many are often attributed to former First Lady Mamie Eisenhower. One of my fond memories is the opportunity my mother and I had to visit the lovely Eisenhower farm near Gettysburg, PA. A story I particularly enjoyed from that tour was how Mamie regularly instructed one of her Secret Service detail to watch her favorite soap opera and let her know what happened, should she miss the show while away or otherwise engaged. No mention was made of Mamie's fudge.

Most sources indicate that fudge seems to be an American concoction from the 1880s, a result of a mistake made with a batch of caramels, and research points to Baltimore as the origin. My friend Kim Gray is a lifelong resident of Baltimore and says that fudge is extremely popular there. She describes Baltimore as a candy city, saying it's no wonder, considering the first U.S. sugar refinery was opened there in 1796.

The Northwest Fudge Factory in Levack, Ontario holds the world record for making the largest slab of fudge. After a week of preparation, the slab came in at a weight of 5,760 pounds and was a mixture of flavor sections including chocolate, vanilla, and maple.

I'm not sure of the source of my mother's peanut butter fudge recipe. As early as I can remember, she made it every Christmas. At times, she packaged it as gifts for friends. I was never satisfied that she only made it at Christmas, and one time as a pre-teen when my mom wasn't home, I decided to make it myself. I actually did a good job, with the exception of using Crisco to "grease" the pan instead of butter.

The recipes for Million Dollar Fudge and Peanut Butter Marshmallow Fudge that I'm sharing here are fairly easy and not overly involved, unlike the Gray family recipe which Kim says, "takes forever, and many a saucepan gave its life for this sugary delight. My sister almost burned our house down making this one Christmas Eve!" Kim is a fascinating storyteller and writer.

Many blessings to you this Christmas, and happy fudge making.

Million Dollar Fudge

Ingredients

2 c semisweet chocolate chips	1 tsp vanilla extract
12 oz. baking chocolate (semisweet or German sweet), broken into small pieces	4-1/2 c granulated sugar
	1 pinch salt
	1 can (12-oz) evaporated milk
	2 T butter
2 small jars (7 oz. each) marshmallow crème	2 c coarsely chopped walnuts

Directions

1. Butter a 9x13 baking dish and set aside.

2. Place chocolates, marshmallow crème, and vanilla in a large bowl and set aside.

3. In large pan, combine sugar, salt, butter, and evaporated milk and bring to a full rolling boil over medium-high heat. Boil for 1 minute, then reduce heat to low/medium-low and cook at a fast simmer for 7 minutes, stirring continuously. Do not scrape the sides of the pan.

4. Pour boiling syrup over chocolate mixture in large bowl and stir vigorously until well combined and smooth. Stir in nuts.

5. Pour into the prepared dish. Let stand at room temperature until firm. Cut into 1-inch squares. Store in airtight container in refrigerator.

Freezes well.

Peanut Butter Marshmallow Fudge

Ingredients

4 c granulated sugar
1 can (12 oz) evaporated milk (Carnation is best)
1/4 lb butter
12 oz marshmallow crème
12 oz smooth peanut butter

Directions

1. Butter a jelly roll pan or sided cookie sheet and set aside.

2. Put marshmallow crème and peanut butter in a large heat-proof bowl and set aside.

3. Combine sugar, evaporated milk, and butter in heavy bottomed saucepan. Bring to boil over medium heat, stirring frequently. Reduce heat to medium-low and continue cooking, stirring often without scraping the sides of pan.

4. Cook until the soft ball stage, 235 F degrees. (Or pour a small amount of the bubbling syrup into a bowl of very cold water. In the water, use your fingers to try to form the syrup into a ball. If it holds a ball shape, it has reached the proper temperature.)

5. Pour liquid over peanut butter and marshmallow crème. Quickly beat by hand until thoroughly mixed. Pour into buttered pan and cool completely. Cut into squares.

Keeps well in airtight container in refrigerator. Also freezes well.

Acknowledgments

Thank you to the Secret Ladies Murder Society, the best grouping of friends and support system, ever.

My deepest gratitude to Demi Stevens, whose skilled support and loving encouragement realizes dreams.

To Aunt Vi's girls, my "sisters" Barb, Debbie, Janice, and Pam—I love and appreciate you.

My ever-abiding love and gratitude to my generous, kind, and supportive husband Craig and our wonderful, sweet family.

About the Author

DENISE WEAVER, a *summa cum laude* graduate of the University of Pittsburgh, is a freelance writer and former library director. She combines her love of sharing food and stories with a penchant for photography and research as inspiration for her writing.

Denise has more than 275 nonfiction articles published in local and regional magazines, most of which focus on food. She also has essays and a short story published in the Mindful Writers Retreat anthology series.

Denise and her husband enjoy traveling and exploring local foods. They split their time between homes in the beautiful Laurel Highlands of Pennsylvania and the irresistible Sunshine State. They have a wild child in the form of a two-year-old Golden Retriever, plus four much better-behaved grown children, their spouses, and two grandsons.